A BOOK OF
BLESSINGS

Glynn is one of my oldest friends. He has been a blessing in my life - mostly. In this beautiful collection of blessings, he sees - and puts into words - with simplicity and skill, the ordinary and the obvious which go unnoticed but speak to the human condition and capacity, frailty and courage. They speak too of the many gifts we enjoy in the world in which we live and the creatures we are privileged to share life with.

Enjoy these words, use them wisely. They will illuminate and disturb and bless you as they have me.

Archbishop Philip Richardson
Archbishop of New Zealand
Bishop of Waikato and Taranaki

Glynn Cardy's blessings will take you on a remarkable and surprising journey through life's amazing paradoxes from zany joy to crushing grief - and always compassion. Nothing is excluded but even the most creative mind cannot be comprehensive. The blanks invite the reader to discover yet more blessedness. Glynn's mind is heaven and earthbound - but, reader, (or pray-er, if pray is what you do) unearth or reach up to add your own. With or without the god of your imagination, go on this blessed pilgrimage and, if you must, add your curses. You would have the Bible on your side.

Paul Oestreicher,
Canon Emeritus of Coventry Cathedral
Anglican/Quaker peace and human rights campaigner

Glynn Cardy's blessings are created from a place of profound attentiveness to the presence of the sacred in the midst of the ordinary. These blessings come not from the clouds but from kitchens, couches, and everyday companions, resourcing those who seek an earthed and embodied Spirit.

In blessing that which may be judged mundane, Glynn invites us to see differently and so to live more compassionately.

And lest you think that blessings are only for the pious or the dogmatic, be assured these blessings will let you be who you are, respecting your truth and calling you deeper into life.

Margaret Mayman
Minister at St Michael's Uniting Church, Melbourne.

A BOOK OF

BLESSINGS

— GLYNN CARDY —

COVENTRY
PRESS

Published in Australia by
Coventry Press
33 Scoresby Road
Bayswater VIC 3153

ISBN 9781922589019

Catalogue-in-Publication entry is available from the National Library of Australia
http://catalogue.nla.gov.au

Cover design by Ian James – www.jgd.com.au
Text design by Coventry Press
Typeset in Fontin

Printed in Australia

Contents

1

Bless all those who knit

Bless all those who knit,
who sit and click the needles,
bringing the threads together,
into a new creation.

Bless all those who unpick
the holey ideas of yesterday
that no longer serve us well,
unravelling prejudice.

Bless all those who then re-knit
the residue of the past with
the dreams of today into
a new garment of hope.

May we be knitters and un-pickers,
determined and dreamers,
fools, lovers, and conspirators
in this glorious insurrection.

2

Blessed are the cartoonists

Blessed are the cartoonists
and all practitioners of the art of critique,
who produce a smile and a challenge.

Blessed are the baristas
and all practitioners of the art of hospitality,
gently drawing froth our conversations.

Blessed are the cellists
and all who nurture and feed the soul,
playing while something silently stirs within.

Blessed are the disobedient
and all who practise the art of defiance,
in the cause of equality, equity, and equipoise.

Blessed are those who make their bed,
others' beds, and cheerfully clean up mess.
Our environment doesn't beautify itself.

Blessed are those who draw, tamp, play,
rebel, and tidy for, like us, they are
practising building a better world.

3

Blessed are the forgetful

Blessed are the forgetful:

> who didn't remember the muffins until
> the acrid smell crept up the corridor;

> who didn't remember her name
> though you'd known her all your life.

Blessed are the clumsy:

> who knocked the edge of the table
> decorating the carpet with milk;

> whose balance went sideways
> and so did the cake, candles burning.

Blessed are the foolish:

> who tried to say something eminently sensible
> and an embarrassing nonsense came forth;

> who got the wrong end of the stick and
> splintered in their self-esteem.

And blessed are we when forgetful,
>> clumsy
>>> or foolish,
knowing that we are one of many, nay of a multitude,
who trip their way through life, embracing
the floor as it comes up to meet us.

4

Blessed are the lost and found

Blessed are the lost and found,
the minutiae we mislay then seek
– like keys, wallets, socks –
in hiding when needed.
And blessed is St Anthony.

Yet loss is a part of our living,
our prayer, our parties –
saying farewell to what's been,
and what can't be replaced,
even by blessed St Anthony.

Losing is part of finding
what we value, expect,
want, need, and are.
Lost is not the opposite of found,
but part of the journey.

Blessed are we when we lose and find
that our treasure is not in coin,
counts, status, or stature,
but in finding the simplicity
and serenity of joy.

5

Blessed are the puddles

Blessed are the puddles,
the muddy, broad ones on the road,
ones that aren't too deep,
the ones you can easily splosh in.

Blessed is the rain
that makes the puddles,
calling us, beckoning us outside
to share in the deliciousness of deluge.

Blessed are the gumboots,
wonders that wrap our feet,
helpful when there are stones
under the muddy surface.

God of puddles
delighting in the adventurous
abandon of children and adults,
bless us in the communion of splosh.

6

Blessed are the sick

Blessed are the sick,
for time has slowed
and its demands fade.
Self-reliance, always an illusion,
now has a wide fissure
running through it.

Blessed are those who hold you,
those angels of mercy
who cradle you in affection
as you fade, revive, doze,
demand, shiver, sleep, and
seek the relief of distraction.

Blessed is the presence of memories,
solace in the wee hours,
the joys of past come again.
And blessed is remembering
those far from and near to you
offering the presence of their love.

Sickness is part of living
and part of dying,
part of being cared for,
and part of knowing how to care.

7

Blessed are those that gather

Blessed are those that gather.
No security check.
No morality check.
No financial cheque.
Come, as you are.

Blessed are those that gather
for breakfast on the beach.
Ambience is everything.
Everything is here,
needing you.

Blessed are those that gather,
engulfed by the aromas,
by the eclectic tension of
unconditional hospitality –
available with all.

Blessed are those that gather
and discover the "other",
going by many names,
closer than our breathing,
as distant as our fears.

god is the giver.
god is the guest.
god is the grace.
god is the grub.
god is gift.

8

Blessed are they who meet joy

Blessed are they who meet joy
in the simple things - like waking up,
pulling the curtains to greet the day,
the pause before words or caffeine...
and are thankful.

Blessed are they who discover joy
in the complex things - like algebraic
equations, Cyrillic languages,
settling intergenerational disputes...
and give thanks.

Blessed are they who find joy
in playgrounds and cafes,
in waiting rooms and classrooms,
even in queues and crowded malls...
and let thankfulness arise.

Blessed are they who have touched joy -
a vibrating, resurgent energy in
the bush and its streams and creatures,
felt its presence course through them...
and are deeply grateful.

Blessed are they who have heard joy -
in the play of music and merriment,
of laughter and little kindnesses,
of the sea and its many sounds...
and are awash with gratitude.

Blessed are we who have been met,
discovered, found, touched, and
heard by joy; and cannot remain the same.
We are the thankful.
We are the blessed.

9

Blessed are those now at rest

Blessed are those now at rest
who stood up
when contemporaries
sat compliant and bowed to
bullies and riches.

Blessed are those now at rest
who loved and lost,
were shattered,
yet found courage to love and,
maybe, lose again.

Blessed are those now at rest
who ate poverty
with loneliness,
praying and scheming for
a better day.

Blessed are those now at rest
who when drained by
despair, disillusion,
began the hard long road
back to happy.

Joy is glimpsed when trying
to hold to what is
ultimately true:
love, friendship, justice –
and not just for a few.

Blessed are those now at rest
who stood up,
who found courage,
who prayed and schemed,
and who began the long road home
to joy.

10

Blessed are those that move over

Blessed are those that move over,
who shuffle their chairs along,
so others can fit around the table.

Blessed are those who serve out the food,
making sure everyone has enough,
including the latecomers.

Blessed are those who shift their positions
when comfortable, certain, and safe,
to accommodate others and their ideas.

Blessed are those that seek to redistribute,
making sure that everyone gets enough,
so that hunger and privilege will be no more.

For this planet is a big round table
with room for all, even the bad and mad.
There are no borders unless we build them.

11

Blessed are those unheralded souls

Blessed are those unheralded souls who slip
tangentially into situations,
coaxing forth possible solutions;
and who, on the edges, help and restore.

Blessed are those who seek the common good
even when it's not their own;
caring for those who don't care for them,
caring for those who can't or won't be good.

Blessed are those who've learnt and give empathy
without needing reciprocity,
without needing recognition or reward.
They emanate contentment – like angels.

Blessed are those tireless encouragers,
who see the best in the worst,
who see the light in the cracks of our lives,
who lead us, guide us, bring us home to our heart.

12

Blessed are those who are afraid

Blessed are those who are afraid
yet still open the door,
who keep on believing things
could be different.

Blessed are those who knock
on the doors that are shut,
who keep on quietly persisting
with their presence.

Blessed is the glimmer of hope
that gets in through the cracks,
gently inviting us to put aside
our misgivings and fear.

Blessed are those who pray
that they will be led to somewhere
good – even to acceptance,
even to friendship.

Blessed are those who understand
that faith is not certainty,
but living with uncertainty,
and with courage.

13

Blessed are those who are late

Blessed are those who are late,
irritatingly late,
who are on time in their own time,
while we wait.

Blessed are those who are loud,
irritatingly loud,
who turn up the volume so our silence
is drowned.

Blessed are those who make mess,
irritating mess,
who freely splatter their living
blind to our misgivings.

Blessed are those who with anarchic doings
irritate our ordered living.

We hate such irritation,
reminders of what we keep hidden
out of sight, under control –
we hope.

So bless them.
And may we have patience both
with them and that part of us
we see in them.

14

Blessed are those who can open

Blessed are those who can open
their doors, tables, and hearts,
letting the known and unknown
come in.

Blessed are those who absorb
others' quirks, hurts, and foibles,
with good humour and calm;
gracefully.

Blessed are those hosts who know
that they are in turn welcome and
needed, as they welcome and
feed others.

Blessed are those hosted who know
and appreciate the vulnerability that such
welcome might bring. Respect goes
both ways.

Blessed are we when we open,
absorb, welcome, need, feed, appreciate,
and allow others to gently return
the same.

15

Blessed are those who don't have religion

Blessed are those who don't have religion,
who might want to
but don't
can't
won't
believe.

Blessed are those who don't try
to convince those irreligious
who don't
can't
won't
otherwise.

Blessed are those who believe they
could be wrong
about much
most
nearly
everything.

And blessed are those who in finding
they are wrong
stop
look
change
once again.

16

Blessed are those who hold hands

Blessed are those who hold hands:
walking on a path, up a hill;
sharing, kneading, baking memories
with affection.

Blessed are those who hold hands:
friends tenderly touching, gifting,
restoring, comforting, and saying,
'I'm here'.

Blessed are those who hold hands:
as one dies and the other cries;
the silence between saying all
that's needed.

Blessed are those who hold hands:
offering a mysterious energy,
balm for the journey into
the unknown.

Blessed are we whose hands are held.

17

Blessed are those who know when to give up

Blessed are those who know when to give up,
when to walk away, to surrender.
In the world of profit and loss,
loss gets a bad rap,
and love does not appear
on balance sheets.

Blessed are those who find meaning,
purpose, and joy to fill the gap
between birth and death;
though sometimes they find us,
and come to us unexpectedly
like a stray cat.

Blessed are those sane enough to lose well,
to let go of striving, to listen to their heart,
to allow others to care for them,
to smell the aroma of goodwill,
to know that failure is fleeting,
and aroha* is forever.

May you be blessed with a good dying:
when all that needs to be said is said,
when all that needs to be done is done,
when all that needs to be felt is felt,
when worries have melted away
and the warmth of love holds you fast.

aroha is a Māori word for love of others, compassion.

18

Blessed are those who let go

Blessed are those who let go,
let be.

Let go, let be,
is a practice of peace,
of minding the soul,
best done with
a community.

Little worries can niggle
their way inside,
into the heart and
in the face we offer
to others.

Let go, let be,
is not dissociative
but associative,
becoming one
with many.

Busyness is an
infectious disease
blinding us to
the unexpected stranger,
the strange.

Let go, let be,
is a great ideal
but needs practice,
like a child with
a piano.

May we let go, let be,
into all that awaits
just around the corner
offering arms filled
with grace.

Blessed are those who let go,
let be.

19

Blessed are those who love without why

Blessed are those who
love without why.
Love doesn't need a reason.
And if it did, is it
love?

Blessed are those who
live without why.
No reason. Just living for the joy
of it. Appreciative.
Content.

Blessed are those who
work without why.
Making, creating. It's just
what they do. Like a rose
blooming.

Blessed are we when we are in
our true home, in compassion,
in the love that doesn't need a reason
but is the healing of
the world.

20

Blessed are those who read to children

Blessed are those who read to children,
and those who help children to read.
Reading opens windows.

Blessed are those who provide children with security:
to inquire, be confident, and take risks.
Nesting nurtures flight.

Blessed are those who encourage children to climb,
to enjoy making huts, scrambling up and swinging in trees.
Trees care for us.

Blessed are those who play with children,
who kick off their shoes, giggle, and enter imaginary worlds.
Children lead us into God.

21

Blessed are those who know the joy

Blessed are those who know
the joy of a friend, parent, or child,
who accept us without rhyme
or reason or reward,
who love us with a power
that can withstand the assault
of our doubt.

Blessed are those who fall
into the embrace of love,
into the losing of doubt,
the choosing of delight,
the wonder and the pain
of acceptance, without
thought of gain.

Blessed are those who awake
to the gift, the giving;
awake into something other
and surprisingly without conditions.
How strange is this?
Isn't love like gold, needing
to be paid for?

Blessed are those who refuse
to succumb or collude
with the lies about love,
that it has to be earnt or

a skill to be learnt;
and we should be grateful like
a beneficiary "should".

Blessed are those who give
freely, unreservedly, all the love,
respect, and strength they can,
generously, without restraint.
Love is like the rain – it falls,
refreshes, sustains, flows...
watering our souls.

22

Blessed are those who sit listening

Blessed are those who sit listening,
with a heart of solace and support,
to the wounded friend skewered
by nastiness.

Blessed are those who endure that pain,
prey to the needs of the hurting hurtful,
carrying on being hopeful, in the absence
of hope.

One of the great questions that I would
ask the God I don't believe in is:
'Why are people nasty and hurtful?'
'Why?'

Blessed are those who always see the best
in any situation, joyously optimistic,
who pick us up, make us laugh, play us
a new song.

Blessed are we who sit listening.

23

Blessed are those who stop

Blessed are those who stop
when the lights turn amber.
Why risk, why rush, when life
is in the slowness.

Blessed are those who stop
when the sky turns amber,
whether at dusk or dawn,
and pause to listen.

Blessed are those who know
how to attune the ear
to the needs of the heart,
the beat of Earth.

Blessed are those who know
that the silence, the devices off,
the appointments paused,
invite wisdom in.

24

Blessed are those whose friends aren't dying

Blessed are those whose friends aren't dying.
May you enjoy the summer of life without
worrying about that dark winter
of time running away.

Blessed are those whose friends are dying slowly,
having time to laugh and remember,
to get used to the horizon's shadow,
and say goodbye.

Blessed are those who are dying themselves,
making time to spin tales, weave kindness,
repair the frayed edges of love,
and even be thankful.

Blessed are we if we can find that our dying
is not a tragic end to be feared,
but a late season to be walked
with a few friends beside.

25

Blessed are we that ache

Blessed are we that ache
in our bones, joints, and muscles,
reminders that we need to move.
Movement means we are alive.

Blessed are we that ache
in our hearts, the centre of our beings,
where rivulets of care turn
the waterwheels generating compassion.

Blessed are we that ache
in our minds, places of meeting with
all manner of life, visible or not, where
disconnection/disintegration threaten.

Aching is a prelude to moving,
to caring, to connecting.
It is a prayer, a blessing,
an annunciation.

26

Blessed are you who awake into stillness

Blessed are you who awaken into stillness,
slowly entering the day...
letting the light gently bathe you with its gift,
as you give thanks for the rest you've had.

Blessed are you who awake into the realisation
that you are loved,
that you are worthy of love, always have been,
even if you don't currently feel it.

Blessed are you who awake into the memory
of happiness and smiles,
from strangers, family, friends, and animals,
and allow those smiles to kindle hope within.

Blessed are you who awake into the possibility
that you are here to help,
to touch another's fragility with your own,
and in that moment both lives are enriched.

Lie still, pushing away anxiety, and listen.
Time is not a clock with an alarm
but a moment of awareness, of blessedness.

27

Blessed be all us crazies

Blessed be all us crazies,
who like sploshing in puddles,
singing in the shower
and wearing indigo to breakfast.
Let's celebrate crazy!

Blessed be all us crazies,
who live a divergent creed:
that difference is good,
that dissent is good,
and that we are good.

Blessed be all us crazies,
risking our reputations welcoming
in the least and the worst,
loving even the unrepentant,
and leaving none behind.

Blessed be all us crazies,
of whatever place, faith, or race,
who dream, hope, and work for
a world without walls and wars,
worries and wrongs.

28

Blessed be socks

Blessed be socks,
woven, woollen, warm,
wrapping our needy feet.

Blessed be socks,
especially when sitting still
feeling the cold seep in.

Blessed be socks,
protecting our fragile toes,
means of mobility and stability.

Blessed be socks,
colourful, variegated, distinct,
or dreary, bland, unnoticeable.

Blessed be socks.
May we learn to value what
we wear for granted.

29

Blessed be sunlight through green leaves

Blessed be sunlight through green leaves,
dappled radiance, filtered glory.
Time to pause, look, and wonder.

Blessed be the smell of a warming drink,
afternoon incense, tonic for the weary.
Time to inhale, sip, and ponder.

Blessed be the lure of a good book,
massaging the mind, catching the novel.
Take time to let the mind meander.

Blessed be the slow time needed
for wondering, pondering, and meandering.
A sacred, holy watch.

30

Blessed be the undone

'I am undone.' Soren Kierkegaard

Blessed be the undone,
mischievous laces ready to trip,
needing us to stop
and attend.

Blessed be the undone,
bereft of bankable certainties,
following an insistent whisper
into the mist.

Blessed be the undone,
buttons missing holes, body
peeping out, snagging
our attention.

Blessed be the undone,
heart-pierced, cold misery.
Our body attending to
the pain.

Blessed be the undone,
lost in the labyrinths of demand,
who find a mystical thread
deep within.

31

Blessed be the whisper

Blessed be the whisper
often hard to hear
but there regardless
every day.

Every day do you hear it?
It's coming from the path.
It's coming from the cup.
It's coming from the mirror.

When you walk,
when you drink,
why your very looks...
it whispers.

It whispers quietly, disturbingly:
you are infused with divinity –
tiny, tender, terrifying...
every day.

Blessed be the whisper
that suggests all is not as it seems,
that around the corner of our banality
our brilliance awaits.

*'God [is] a cup in your house that you haven't yet recognised as God
but you drink from nearly every day.' Jack Underwood*

32

Blessed be this home

Blessed be this home
where we can learn to be
strong, weak, and safe.

Blessed be our kitchen table,
centre of our gathering,
our talking, our laughter.

Blessed be our food,
edible, spiritual, life-giving,
sustaining togetherness.

Blessed be the mediators
who help us with others'
vulnerabilities and with our own.

Blessed be the grumpy,
for the confidence to tell us
how they feel, and we them.

Blessed be those who notice
the messes in our lives, and in
their messiness offer love to help.

Blessed be the clowns,
those who play and fool around,
leavening our lives and wellbeing.

Blessed be this home
where we can learn to be
strong, weak, and safe.

33

Blessed be those who know the silence

Blessed be those who know
the silence of wisdom;
the silence of humility;
the silence of love...
the silence without the need of words –
the silence of being at one.

Blessed be those who know
to silence the drums of demand;
to silence their appetites;
to silence their needs; their greed;
and to listen for the whisper of compassion,
and hear its haunting quiet.

Blessed be those who know.
Blessed be those who try.
Blessed be those who for a moment
enter the deep silence,
feeling the pain and despair of loss
from which the phoenix might come.

34

Blessed be those who mourn

Blessed be those who mourn
who enter the nothingness
who remember slowly...
who, in time, turn their hands
ready to touch and be touched, again.

Blessed are the dead who go
and yet remain, lingering,
tending our memories
as we turn to the hurting
who await our ears and hands and passion.

Blessed are those who rage
against all that sucks out joy –
those destructive deeds
and indifference; for holy anger can
seed and water a deep resilience, resurgence.

Blessed are those who give birth
to beautiful blossoms of hope:
kind words, smiles, quiet chuckles,
a place for all where wounds are tended,
and justice and joy lovingly embrace.

35

Blessed is a poem

Blessed is a poem
the verses of which are still being written,
as we discover who we are
and might become.

Blessed is a symphony
in which we are invited to play,
but in which the music keeps changing...
so we improvise.

Blessed is a work of art
forming with the colours and strokes we bring,
transforming us as it emerges, changing
how we see.

Blessed is a silence,
a gap, a pause between words,
a waiting, a holding, a patience, a stillness
as the tide recedes.

Blessed is the elusive divine,
moving within and without, beyond,
paradoxical, questionable, a mystery,
a child playing.

36

Blessed is a slice of gingerbread

Blessed is a slice of gingerbread
topped with thick butter,
a soul gift for the sick or weary,
symbol of solace.

Blessed are those who express
their love in culinary deeds,
their attention to detail
a gift of care.

Blessed is a fresh cinnamon brioche,
the aroma mingling with the coffee,
served with tender presence,
a welcome gift.

Blessed is a loaf of gingerbread
still warm from the baking,
ready for the nexus, the re-forming
of friendship.

37

Blessed is a welcoming doorway

Blessed is a welcoming doorway
exuding light and warmth.
But is this pleasing frame
all that it seems?

Blessed is an invitation to step
over the sill, without tripping,
but ready none-the-less to be
seen as a fool.

Blessed are the doorways that lead
to the broadening of mind and soul.
But are we ready to relinquish
customs we cherish?

Blessed are the courageous fools
who step into the different,
stumbling, recovering, then entering
frames not of their making.

38

Blessed is the one in the middle

Blessed is the one in the middle
of a bridge as it sways
breathing in the space
below, above, and beyond,
who says a prayer, a sigh,
grateful for it all.

Blessed is the one in the middle
of the kitchen as mixtures
bake, bubble, simmer, sizzle,
mystery and magnificence
perfume the air, inviting,
an oblation to Rongo.*

Blessed is the one in the middle
of the Holden's backseat,
feeling that 'together vibe',
going on a ride, an adventure,
to who knows or cares where,
with those we trust.

Blessed is the one in the middle
of the church, alone, feeling
the ambience, memories, meanings
laid in this kiln of intoxicating kindness,
a place for firing the heart
a home for the soul.

Blessed are we in the middle
of life, of living, of divinity...
of joy, of grief, of hope...
swaying, baking, riding...
being, feeling, loving...
making prayer.

Rongo is a Māori deity of cultivated foods.

39

Blessedness is something found unexpectedly

Blessedness is something
found unexpectedly when
distraction causes us to pause.

May the gracious be blessed
as they hold both the bruised
and the bruising in their compass.

May the impure be blessed
knowing that we are all
unfinished works of art.

May the confused be blessed
with an encouraging song
and its soothing spirit.

May the gentle be blessed
protected from grinding demands,
as they wait upon the diminished.

May the sick be blessed
with both care and company,
sensitive and unobtrusive.

May the dismayed be blessed
with the gift of patience
and the spur of impatience.

May the sore be blessed
with a shower of kindness,
an empathetic distraction.

May the dying be blessed
by those who watch with them
held in their own time.

These so blessed, and many more,
hold out to us fragments
of the heaven called hope.

40

Blessed is the simple Christmas

Blessed is the simple Christmas:
song, story, and prayer,
memories mixed and made...
sustaining fare.

Blessed is the simple table
with everyone there,
sharing food and talk,
laughs and care.

Blessed are the simple things:
hope, helping, the heart,
giving to each other
trust, a new start.

Blessed is the simple truth:
humans are family not a race,
bound by kindness and love,
a gentling grace.

41

How blessed it would be

How blessed it would be
if all activity stopped,
all phones were silent,
and we heard nothing but our breath...
a Sabbath full stop.

Would panic ensue?
Would fear erupt?
Would warning bells ring,
and the markets crash?
Or would a great relief flood our soul?

'Be still, and in the stillness know,'
said the psalmist,
that divinity is the same:
still and silent
and wondrous.

So let us wonder now, together,
of the sublimity of this dear Earth,
of the necessity of courage and faith,
and of the music of intimacy and mutuality,
the blessedness that draws all together.

42

May an Irish blessing be upon you

May an Irish blessing be upon you,
finding happiness in company,
shedding tears in common,
knowing that saint and sinner
are one in us,
and we in them.

May the history not be forgotten,
but the hate subside into longing,
for we are all fragile beneath,
and seek belonging,
a trinity with god,
a unity of all.

May we find shelter.
May we find welcome.
May we find joy in our souls.
May we be found by the god
of fiddle music, tatties,
and belly laughs.

And may we find peace –
both the tranquil kind,
and the troubling kind –
in our weave of pain and joy,
worries and longing,
life and faith.

And may it suffice.

43

May the blessing of a shelter be ours

May the blessing of a shelter be ours,
a place that finds us when the turbulence of loss
seeks to throw us, tip us, tumble us,
and leave us laid low, forlorn, and alone.

May the blessing of a grace inhabit that shelter,
someone who will offer us timely comfort,
a touch of kindness, a cup of calm,
and be there as our souls' fractures mend.

May the blessing of serenity when life is askew,
spinning, wobbling, collapsing... find us too;
a word, a look, a smile that reaches into our misery
and offers us a staff to hold (your hand maybe).

May the blessing of the litter of hope be blown
into that shelter, confetti of long-ago memories,
when that exuberant pup called optimism
demanded our participation, and we played.

May the blessing of a soft light find us,
offering, in our frightened and insecure moments
(moments we hide well), a home to head towards,
where we can lay down pretence and be loved.

And may shelter, grace, serenity, hope, and soft light,
surround us and scatter the chilling darkness
of the long and lonely night.

(Last verse is adapted from ANZPB-HKMOA. Used by permission.)

44

May we be blessed by a foolishness

May we be blessed by a foolishness
that believes the divisions that tear our world
can be overcome, that hate can be healed,
and we can live in harmony.

May we be blessed by a forgiveness,
received and given, for the conspiratorial ways
we keep the gates of our privilege closed,
lest the least get within.

May we be blessed by a fearlessness,
a courageous counter-intuitive form of faith,
that imagines and acts to bring to birth
the fragile gift of hope.

May we be that fool.
May we be that open.
May we be that hope.
May we be the blessing we seek.

45

Blessed be joy

Blessed be joy,
the pattern that connects,
that radiates within and without,
fracturing the bounds
that compartmentalise.

Joy tumbles, giggles, flows,
spilling out, gushing up and over,
and saturating our lives,
irrevocably changing us.
It is our river.

Joy is the vast living ocean
in which we swim, float, dive,
essential to planetary life.
It is wild and calm,
restorative.

Joy is the endless sky
in which we gaze and marvel,
of which we are a part,
the whole of which is in us,
light and dark.

Sacred luminous joy,
shine brightly, energising all,
kindle kindness and compassion,
stir wonder and appreciation.
You are our healer.

46

May we be blessed with a book

May we be blessed with a book,
the words of which are being written
in the way we live.

May we be blessed with eyes to read,
with hearts to hear, and minds to discern
what might be true.

May a suspicious spirit bless us,
holding up all texts to the judgment
of just love and kind acts.

And may the flow of divine goodness,
that bursts the banks of the written word
carry us, sustain us, and refresh us.

47

May we be blessed with contentment

May we be blessed with contentment –
having enough, caring enough, being loved enough.
And may this contentment seed and spread.

May we be blessed with vulnerability –
to feel the pain of others, and to recognise our own.
And may this vulnerability keep us in touch.

May we be blessed with wild joy – that
irrational impulse to laugh or dance or sing whenever.
And may this wild joy join us with the heartbeat of god.

May contentment, vulnerability, and wild joy
be our companions on the paths before us.

48

Blessed are we when the old light lessens

Blessed are we when
the old light lessens
and our thoughts darken,
and we find ourselves bereft.
All we leaned on has fallen,
the world of certainty is crumbling.

Blessed are we when
in that twilight gloom,
steadying ourselves momentarily,
we imagine there is a new light,
carefully nurtured by love,
within us, hard to see, but there.

Blessed are we when
this dawning light speaks,
telling us we're not alone,
that there are other lights,
all seeking to shine forth
and lessen our suffering.

Blessed are we when
with closed eyes, we corral
our wayward worries, and
open ourselves to the wonder,
kindness, and saving grace
of this matrix of light.

49

May you be blessed with a restless discomfort

May you be blessed
with a restless discomfort
about easy answers, half-truths,
and superficial relationships,
so that you may seek truth
and love deep within your heart.

May you be blessed
with holy anger at injustice,
oppression, and exploitation of people,
so that you may work tirelessly
for justice, freedom,
and empowerment for all.

May you be blessed
by the gift of tears to shed
with those who suffer from pain,
or the loss of all they cherish,
so that you may reach out
your hand to comfort them.

May you be blessed
with enough foolishness to believe
that you really can make a difference,
so that you are able,
with grace and kindness,
to do what others claim cannot be done.

50

May you be blessed with a bridge

May you be blessed with a bridge,
to help you from here to there,
over the uncertainties that gnaw at
your soul.

May it be a fragile bridge,
not a big sturdy one that trumpets
strength or anaesthetises
your pain.

May you have company on that bridge,
fellow seekers of sanity and serenity,
familiar with loss you are
not alone.

And may you find in the walking,
the joy of being, happiness, that can
warm those you love and bring
you home.

Hope is a fragile bridge,
as is the courage to walk it.

'Wisdom (can) come with age and life and pain. And knowing what matters.' Louise Penny

Steve Bradley Photography

51

Blessed is the space of waiting

Blessed is the space of waiting,
the time before the sun awakes,
when the day ahead cannot yet be seen,
and the night's wounds are gated.

Pain and suffering are indiscriminate,
they have no guiding moral compass,
they curse the good and bad alike,
they come to us unbidden.

Blessed is the space of not knowing,
before the confluence of fates and fears
flood our little patch of safety,
and we are immersed in it.

We are both prepared and anxious
for this moment when our resources,
our resolve, and maybe our sanity,
will be tested and suffer.

Blessed is the unexpected aroha,*
the bonds of solidarity that emerge –
the kind thoughts, the helping hands,
that reach out to our need.

Mostly the banks of hope hold.
Maybe there will be life after,
maybe we will survive,
maybe the dawn will come again.

*aroha is a Māori word for love of others, compassion.

52

Blessed is our mother Earth

Blessed is our mother Earth
when she knows that she is deeply loved,
not a 'thing', a 'resource', to be used,
but our papakainga,*
our only home.

Blessed is our mother Earth
when indifference is countered by passion,
and the parched and abused ground
is tended by our tears,
and resolve to restore.

Blessed are we when finding
wisdom and courage,
memory and resilience,
and non-compliance,
for the facing of these hours.

papakainga is a Māori word for original home village, home base.

Final verse reflects Verse 1 of God of grace and God of glory by Harry Emerson Fosdick (1878-1969)

53

May the blessing of a child's smile

May the blessing of a child's smile
in this season of spending visit us,
amid the bustle and brashness,
assaulted by unrelenting jolliness,
may it come unheralded to hold
our fragile and weary hearts.

May the blessing of a magic gift,
like a hand when the pain is too much,
like a ginger-loaf when troubles overwhelm,
visit us carolling a hope we don't feel,
in this season of hard memories,
when we are all but spent.

May the blessing of unexpected quiet,
the space between the busyness,
reach out to compass our despair,
and hold us tenderly for a while,
as we relish a moment of serenity,
a guiding star in the pitch of night.

May the blessing of the little,
the hidden, the frail hope of
the weak force of love, touch us
in this time of tinsel reminding
that contrary to what we see
there might be a greater reality.

Heather Chapman Photography

54

May we be blessed with home

May we be blessed with home:
a place, a space, a still point;
a family, a friendship, a fellowship;
a door that will always be unlocked;
a familiar smell and feel;
where our heart is safe;
where we have nothing to prove;
where we welcome visitors;
and where we know the god we breathe.
May all know the blessing of home.

55

May we be blessed with love

May we be blessed with love,
that mysterious and sacred trust:
showing us who we are;
helping us to live in the moment;
teaching us kindness and loyalty;
awakening in us gratitude and grace;
expressing itself as joy and wonder.
May we be blessed by love.

56

May the blessing of stretching your soul

May the blessing of stretching your soul,
out from the strictures of urban demand,
on a clear chilly morning,
watching the sun begin
to rub warmth into the world,
be yours.

May the blessing of the gentle brook,
as it gurgles past your planted feet,
whispering its sacred truths
to the waiting in you
and to all life that it nurtures,
be yours.

May the blessing of the alluring hills,
with pink tops and shadowed sides,
calling to the dreamers,
offering a korowai,*
a cloak of protection and hope,
be yours.

May the blessing of new beginnings,
with all their promises and anxieties,
in the company of fellow
hopers and worriers,
together at this intersection,
be yours.

And may all these blessings –
the stretching soul, the gentle brook,
the alluring hills, the new beginnings –
encourage you to recognise,
then step around your fears,
and walk into the wrap of grace.

korowai is a Māori word for cloak.

57

May we know the blessing of a morning prayer

May we know the blessing of
a morning prayer delivered
by a wet nose and doggy breath.

May we know the blessing of
a night prayer of a furry bundle
settling on our lap.

May we know the privilege of
caring for an animal friend,
and that care being reciprocated.

May we know the presence of god
in smell, in breath, in touch,
in playfulness, in fidelity, in need.

And may we know ourselves
to be blessed.

58

May we know the blessing of peace

May we know the blessing of peace:
peace deep within, peace going without,
and the difficult peace across divisions –
a rickety bridge.

May we know the blessing of *shalom*:
peace that feeds, peace that welcomes;
and peace that bravely allows itself to
be vulnerable.

May we know the blessing of *salaam*:
peace that helps, peace that heals,
and peace that works unseen to
prevent wounding.

May we know the blessing of *filemu*:*
peace that speaks out, peace of silence,
and peace that uses its strength to hold
and empower others.

May we know the blessing of *rangimarie*:*
peace of belonging, peace of building,
and the just peace bridging the chasm
between worlds.

*filemu (Samoan) and *rangimarie (Māori) both mean peace.*

59

May you be blessed with a cat

May you be blessed with a cat
who demands attention,
your affection,
your lap.

May you be blessed with feline
friendship, solace when alone,
the stroking of
your heart.

May you be blessed with offerings
dead on the kitchen floor -
an old language
for thanks.

May you be blessed with the lessons,
of living with a small friend,
one that sheds
and meows.

60

Blessed be grandfathers

Blessed be grandfathers,
watching, waiting, anticipating,
sentinels of patience,
gifting love wrapped in time.

Blessed be grandfathers
who have known loss, met despair,
and yet still smile like the sun,
with their eyes and hearts.

Blessed be grandfathers
soaked in life, aged in wisdom,
with wounds no longer raw,
gracious and gentle.

Blessed be grandfathers
taking pleasure in others' joy,
mending the many cracks
made by demands.

Blessed be grandfathers,
a vocation of being,
ready to be called,
for whom love is all.

And blessed be we
who have known,
and been loved,
by such grandfathers.

Photograph by Alan Hayward

61

May you be blessed with an unruly dog

May you be blessed with an unruly dog,
a hybrid from the pound,
who makes a mess -
like a holey garden
or gnawed furniture.

May you be blessed with a wet tongue
and eager foul breath
one Saturday sleep-in,
compelling you to arise
and grudgingly respond.

May you be blessed with a visit to the vet,
2 a.m. on the far side of town,
after finding the gnawed wrapper
of your favourite chocolate
strewn down the corridor.

May you be blessed with a dog impossible
to walk in canine company
[to say nothing of feline!];
a drag on your patience and fellow
dog-walkers' forbearance.

May you be blessed with being told
that these dog trials are a test
of your character and fortitude,
'one of life's lessons'
that you somehow stood in.

There comes a time when looking
into those dewy eyes you might see
how enmeshed your lives
have become...
and your soul is laid bare.

You might have no idea what this means,
but not even death can part you.

62

Blessed are the Teddy Bears

Blessed are the Teddy Bears,
newly acquired and elegantly attired,
and those long on our journey,
whom love has worn bare.

Blessed are those who love,
through thick, thin, tries, and tragedies,
mud, grease, and the washing machine;
always there when we roll over.

Blessed are the Teddy Bears
with furry arms open wide for hugs
in a world closed up inside for fear
of being hit with heartache, hurt.

Blessed is the unearned, unsought
embrace of Teddy Bears whether
you're poor, pretty, or plain,
conventional, different, or brainy.

Blessed are we Teddy Bears
who counter the fear and hurt of life
with the simplicity and grace
of unconditional love.

63

Blessed are we when resisting temptation

Blessed are we when resisting temptation...

the temptation to do only what we've seen done,
and have it shape our expectations;

the temptation to work for gain but never for loss,
and to believe this is success;

the temptation to love only the lovable – never the despicable,
for we will be tainted by the latter;

the temptation to think that we can't change the big stuff,
and carry on living in quiet despair;

the temptation to ignore the frayed webs
of connectivity between us,
and not strengthen and rebuild them.

Blessed are the resisters.

64

Blessed be doors

Blessed be doors,
big ones and blue,
or round and rainbow; or
ones that look like you.

Blessed be doors,
that open us onto new paths
of thought, being, and acting,
if we walk through.

Blessed be doors,
that attract no attention,
but are there as a pointer
to a different way.

Blessed be doors,
that open when we least expect it,
inviting us into a new place,
suggesting we stay.

And blessed are we
when we do.

65

Blessed be God's verbs

Blessed be God's verbs
in our minds, in our mouths,
in our hearts, in our actions,
and in our connecting.

May the verbs of God:
to love, include, and care,
be our guide and goal
in this time of fear.

May the verbs of God
grow like well-watered tomatoes,
juicy, sumptuous, satisfying,
ready to be shared.

May we be verbs of God:
noticing those out of sight,
hearing those who are silent,
a shelter for those without.

Blessed be God's verbs
in our minds, in our mouths,
in our hearts, in our actions,
and in our connecting.

66

Blessed be beauty

Blessed be beauty.
It is ever-changing,
a fusion – known
when we see it.

Flowers, music,
evocative designs,
all pale before the
magic of a smile.

Light reflects, laughing.
It sparkles, glitters,
dancing on the surface
of the stream.

Water, movement,
our eyes, and light...
An intersection
of wonder.

No thing determines
beauty. It is a play
of the inner on outer,
the outer on inner.

Hint of becoming;
spark of cheekiness;
graced care;
beauty is discovering

ourselves. We are
beautiful. In soul.
In body. In speech.
In thought. Always

a confluence, a smile
a dance, a bridge,
a play, a discovery...
Blest by beauty.

67

Blessed is life

Blessed is life:
life that gives us meaning and hope
when death, and the fear of it, come.
Life is always a transient gift.

Blessed is time:
time to pause what we've been doing
and move to another way of being and doing
– while we still can.

Blessed is fibre:
the mystery of 'net connection helping
the weave of community to continue,
re-form, flourish even.

Blessed is touch:
the touch of family and animals living close,
and the touch of those distant but caring.
Touch feeds the soul.

Blessed is hope:
hope that kindnesses and other acts
will heal the loneliness, anxiety, and suffering;
and we will overcome.

Blessed is all that we take for granted
when so much suddenly can't be.
And blessed are all those who help us
be strong in these times.

68

Blessed is the angel

Blessed is the angel
who alleviates pain,
who showers relief,
who calms our breathing,
and encourages 'this too
will pass'.

Blessed is the angel
who takes the time
to bring practised aid;
anything that will distract
us from the pain that
consumes.

Blessed is the angel
whether fat, fit, or feeble,
colourful or conventional,
with attitude or without,
who, for a little while,
gently helps.

Blessed is the angel
alongside, today unknown,
a prayerful presence,
as we endure this valley,
hoping it may end,
before we do.

69

May we be blessed in remembering mothers

May we be blessed in remembering
the mothers in our lives and faith –
who bore, who nurtured, who risked,
who suffered, who rejoiced...

May we be blessed in remembering
the mothers of our courage and kindness –
who bore, nurtured, risked,
suffered, and rejoiced.

May their best be mingled with our best,
and may that best be enough,
to give hope to a needy world,
and to bring joy to needy hearts.

Kathryn Jones Photography

70

Blessed is a world where the weak

Blessed is a world where the weak
are protected, none go hungry,
and the benefits of life are shared.

Blessed is a world where everyone
is treated with dignity and respect,
and all know a safe place called home.

Blessed is a world where animals
and plants, the land and oceans,
are respected and cherished.

Blessed is a world where peace is grounded
in justice, justice is guided by love,
and love is gifted unconditionally.

Blessed is a world where with courage,
kindness, and grace we stand together,
and create this vision of hope.